ENGLISH
VILLAGE LIFE

KT-510-726

ENGLISH VILLAGE LIFE

PARKGATE
BOOKS

First Published in Great Britain in 1997
by Parkgate Books Ltd, London House, Great Eastern Wharf,
London SW11 4NQ

British Library Cataloguing in Publication Data:
A CIP catalogue record for this book is available from the
British Library.

ISBN 1-85585-331-0

Compiled by Philippa Lewis
Designed by Bill Mason
Printed and bound in Great Britain by
Butler & Tanner Ltd, Frome and London

INTRODUCTION

The photographs in this book are of English village life as it approached a watershed. The period that they cover, from 1920 to the early 1950s, was one in which villages still retained patterns of existence that had been built up over many centuries; but enormous changes were on the way.

Most of the photographs were taken for the pioneering magazine Picture Post, *which brought into focus the minutiae of life in Britain and celebrated regional variations. What comes across in them all, from whatever part of the country, is a strong sense of community, and the existence of a well-established social structure and hierarchy. The self-sufficiency of the villages is also apparent. Each one had its own church and clergyman, school and schoolteacher, shops and tradesmen; the larger ones even had their own policeman.*

There was no need to look to the outside world for entertainment for there were local fairs and festivals, bands and parades, cricket matches and meetings — of the parish council and the Women's Institute. A visit to the nearby town was still an event for many people, particularly during and after the war.

In each of the pictures we see scenes and ways of life that were once familiar but are gone forever from England's villages.

THE VILLAGE STREET

A photograph taken one summer's day in 1935 capturing the tranquil life of an English village: sheep are herded through Histon in Cambridgeshire by a shepherd on his bicycle. At this date most of the villagers would have been dependent on the land for their livelihood.

NORTH AND SOUTH

*A family photographed in a typically northern hill village
in Lancashire, with its cottages of grey stone (above),
contrasted with a scene in the southern village of Letcombe
Bassett in Berkshire, where the cottages are mainly of brick
and thatch (right). The look of a village is determined by
the land on which it is built since most of the buildings are
of local materials: stone or slate from nearby quarries,
brick where there is clay suitable for brickmaking and
cob — mud mixed with grit and straw — in some
areas, such as parts of Devon.*

EAST AND WEST

*A motorbicycle with sidecar is the only
traffic in the village street in Barley,
Hertfordshire, where the sign of the Fox and
Hounds pub stretches all the way across
the road. Here the local building tradition is
weatherboarding and plaster.
A girl walks her dog down a lane in the
village of Laverton in Gloucestershire,
where both walls and roofs are of
golden Cotswold stone.*

COTTAGES

*The archetypal dream cottage with neatly thatched roof
and carefully tended garden, lying in sight of an ancient
church tower and lych-gate. For many villagers, though,
the reality was that their cottages were damp, dark and
dilapidated, and money badly needed to be spent on their
maintenance by the landlord. This family is moving
out of a cottage in Woodmancote, Gloucestershire, at the
end of the Second World War and exchanging it for a
modern prefab built by the council.*

COTTAGE INTERIORS

Two elderly men caught by the camera in the comfort of their homes: seated by the window, with tomatoes ripening on the sash, at Salthouse in Norfolk (above), and practising the euphonium to play in the band at Tinsley in Yorkshire (right). There was a strong tradition of music in the North, particularly in the mining villages.

COUNTRY KITCHENS

Kitchens photographed in the mid-20th century in Essex (above), Bishop's Itchington, Warwickshire (left), and Botallack in Cornwall (right). The women are working in kitchens that would have changed little since the 19th century. As well as being used for cooking, the kitchen range provided heating for the whole house. It was concluded in a report in 1934 that once electricity had been installed the time spent by the housewife on chores in the home was reduced from 26 hours a week to seven.

VILLAGE WOMEN

*Very few women had work outside the
village, their time being fully taken up
with domestic tasks and bringing up
their children. In all rural communities,
though, they were relied on to help at
particularly busy times of year. A
farmer's wife lends a hand with sheep-
shearing in Westmorland (above).*

VILLAGE MEN

Most of the menfolk were employed on the land or with work connected with agriculture. A farm labourer photographed in 1940 (right), when the agricultural wage was £2 8s 3d a week. The vegetable garden (above) was usually the responsibility of the men of the family, while the poultry was looked after by the women.

VILLAGE GIRLS

A girl is taught sewing in the village school. The classes were often segregated, the boys learning woodwork while the girls were taught the domestic sciences. Photographs taken in 1939 and 1940 show that girls were still helping out in the fields and with the stock.

VILLAGE BOYS

*Five boys from the village school in Mells, Somerset,
display their prowess with hand-bells in 1935 (right).
The band was booked to perform 'turns' at local
Christmas concerts. Boys work and play in the
harvest fields in wartime Gloucestershire, riding
the carthorse and playing in the stubble
(above and above right).*

THE VICAR

*A central figure in village society was the vicar, who was
often the best-educated person in the village. As well as
taking regular church services, and christening, marrying
and burying his parishioners, he had to manage the
upkeep of the church, distribute alms, arbitrate in local
disputes and occasionally perform duties such as that of
exorcizing ghosts. He held the respect of the whole village,
and all would tip their hats to him in passing. The rector
takes tea by the light of an oil lamp with a parishioner in
Upton, Lincolnshire. At St Petrock's at Parracombe in
Devon the vicar has a word with members of the
congregation in the porch of his church.*

TH BOBBY

The village bobby had some very different duties from those of a metropolitan policeman. He was, for example, responsible for reporting any notifiable pests or diseases affecting animals and crops, and this Gloucestershire policeman checks on the sheep-dipping to make sure that it is carried out according to regulations. He was also responsible for checking that the licensing laws were correctly observed and that no person rode a cart or wagon upon the King's highway without holding the reins. In some villages the lock-up, where the village constable would detain local miscreants or drunks, can still be seen.

THE CRAFTSMEN

Larger villages were almost self-sufficient, with blacksmiths, carpenters, shoemakers and saddlers all serving the local people. The men were their own masters and so were considered a rung above the agricultural workers who had to look to the local farmers and landowners for employment. Many crafts were associated with particular areas: potters where there was clay, basket-makers where withies grew, and so on. The saddler was photographed in the village of Urchfont in Wiltshire in 1952. The village carpenter was photographed in Essex.

RURAL SKILLS

*Specialist demand: in the hop fields labourers fix the twine
for the hop bines onto the poles — what can now be
performed by machine was in 1927 done on stilts. The
photograph was taken in Waterley, Kent. The skill of the
thatcher was needed to keep thatched cottages watertight.
The thatch had to be renewed every 30 years or so, but
many landlords allowed it to decay to the point where the
cottage quickly deteriorated, especially if the walls were
built of cob.*
This thatcher is at work on the roof of The Ship Inn

TIME TO TALK

The pace of village life and the way in which communities were so closely knit, with people involved in each other's business, meant that there was often time to stand and talk, and discuss matters of moment (below). Two women gossip outside the village shop in Laxton, Nottinghamshire (left). Until the Second World War it was common for country dwellers to spend all their lives in one place and travel no further than the local town.

TIME TO WATCH

For the young and the old there was always something going on in the village to watch: sheep-dipping in Woodmancote in Gloucestershire or a farrier at work near Dorchester in Dorset. Although some farriers travelled around the farms to cold shoe horses, the job was considered much better done at the forge, and there was a blacksmith in most villages.

THE VILLAGE SHOP

The village shop was somewhere to exchange news and gossip, replacing the village pump as the traditional place to gather. A crowded scene in the general store in Salthouse, Norfolk, which could clearly provide everything from scrubbing brushes to sweets. Because many of the goods had to be weighed and measured individually, shopping was apt to be a slow business. Many larger villages would have had their own butcher and baker. The butcher of Shere in Surrey poses outside his shop.

THE VILLAGE SCHOOL

The infants of Lovington in Somerset at prayers in the village school, while those at Westerleigh near Bristol have games in the playground. In the late 1940s and early 1950s every village had a school, however small the attendance roll.

THE VILLAGE PUB

The traditional preserve of the men of the village and somewhere to retreat to for a pint, conversation and maybe a game or a song. A village would often have several pubs, although some might be little more than the front room of a cottage with the beer being drawn from barrels in a separate room. Cards in Kelsale in Suffolk (right), a song in The Eel's Foot in Eastbridge, Suffolk (left), and a lunchtime chat in a pub in the Wye Valley (below).

LOCAL BREWS

Pressing apples for cider in an old cider-press. This farmer near Congresbury in Somerset was photographed in 1944, in which year he expected to press 12,000 gallons of cider between October and Christmas. Many pubs had a licence to brew their own beer. The publican of The Golden Lion at Southwick in Hampshire, where the publican had brewed the beer himself for 40 years when this photograph was taken in 1946.

T H E   V I L L A G E   C H U R C H

*The parish church, at the heart of every village and almost
always its most ancient building, perhaps dating back to
medieval times. Around the church are usually clustered the oldest
houses in the village, and often a pub. This may be a relic of the
ancient holstelry where the stonemasons and other craftsmen
lodged when they were building the church, and where the
churchwardens stored ale for festivals. Spires and towers as a
backdrop to village life: sheep-shearing in the shadow of the 13th-
century church at Easton-in-Gordano in Somerset (right) and
cricket at Wombourne in Staffordshire (above).*

CHRISTENINGS AND WEDDINGS

Relations and godparents grouped around the ancient stone font in the church of St Faith's in Overbury, Worcestershire (left), at which generations of villagers have been baptized. Moments before the christening service begins in 1942, an older woman admires the baby while the mother looks on. Village wedding customs: in the West Country children often tied up the church gate in order to exact a toll from a newly-married couple, as here at Uley (above). On Holy Island (above left) fishermen fire guns over the couple's heads to bring them good fortune.

A VILLAGE AUCTION

A Gloucestershire village in 1954: a cottager dies and his household effects are displayed and then auctioned in the village street. From the unusual number of cars along the road it is clear that people have come from miles around in the hope of finding a valuable antique.

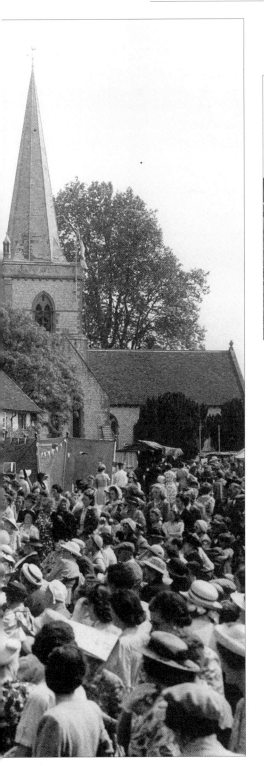

COMMON AND GREEN

*In medieval times cottagers had the right to graze their
animals on common land and collect wood for fuel.
Although this land was gradually enclosed for fields
during the 18th and 19th centuries, it survives in many
villages, and scenes such as this (above) were once
familiar. Whereas common land lies on the edge of the
village, the green lies at its heart. The typical medieval
village was built with the houses facing onto the green,
their gardens and land lying behind. Although over the
centuries buildings have encroached on it, the green has
remained a favourite feature of the village: a stage for any
spectacle, from placing wrong-doers in the stocks and
dancing round the maypole to an event such as this
historical pageant being performed at Brockham Green in
Surrey during the summer of 1951 (left).*

THE VILLAGE PUMP

The village pump on the green at Wark in Northumberland (above), in use as late as 1950. Collecting water was always a job for the women and children, and not surprisingly the pump became a place for conversation and gossip before the hard walk home with the buckets. An earlier photograph (right), taken in Tinley in Yorkshire, shows the publican's wife proudly showing off the village's new petrol pump.

TRANSPORT

*The heyday of rural public transport, when
country buses ran regularly: Aston in Hertfordshire in the
early 1950s. Cars were only for the privileged and the
roads correspondingly peaceful: cattle being gently herded
down a village street by a farmer in a
horse and cart, apparently unworried by the prospect
of oncoming traffic.*

NEWCOMERS

After the Second World War the population of the villages expanded dramatically as the country was seen as a better place to live in than the bomb-torn cities. This caused a shortage of housing, and there was pressure for new homes to be built. Some families took matters into their own hands: Mr and Mrs Steward parked an Ipswich trolley bus in the east Suffolk village of Creeting St Mary in 1952 and hoped that by thatching it they might persuade the authorities to classify it as a cottage. The commuter was another post-war arrival: in the autumn of 1948 Mr David Hull is seen off in the morning by his wife Jane from their village home in Surrey.

COUNCIL AND COMMITTEE

*The elected parish councils of England make decisions that affect
the whole community. This scene (right), photographed in 1951,
shows the council meeting in the village school in Bishop's
Itchington, Warwickshire. Unusually for that date, the council
was composed of six women and only one man. Members of the
village fête committee at Flaunden in Hertfordshire count the
money at the end of the day (above). Events like this were
invariably held to raise money for the upkeep of the village
church, the village hall or the playing fields.*

THE WOMEN'S INSTITUTE

The W. I. was founded in 1915 (in a summerhouse in Anglesey), and by the time these photographs were taken in 1953 membership had reached nearly half a million. The organization provided points of contact between women all over the country and was a powerful lobby for such improvements to rural life as the placing of a telephone box in every village, rural bus services and the supply of mains water. For an annual subscription of 2/6 members were encouraged from all social levels, united in work, friendship and recreation. Country dancing in Eastgate, Co. Durham (below left)), a home-made hat competition in Woodstreet, Surrey (above left), and bringing along the tea-urn in Groombridge, Sussex (above).

SUCCEEDING GENERATIONS

Up until the Second World War it was quite common for families to stay in the same village or area for hundreds of years, as the surnames in parish records, on war memorials and on tombstones show. This photograph taken outside a cottage in 1923 documents five generations of the same family.

DOLES AND CHARITIES

*It is one of the first Christian duties to look after the poor,
and in many English villages there were doles or gifts for
needy parishioners that had been established centuries before.
In 1936, at Minstead in Hampshire (left), the rector gives
out one of the 300 'gallons' of bread in accordance with the
terms of the will of a Mr Brown made 300 years previously.
At the service beforehand he preached a sermon for which he
received 10/-. At Biddenden in Kent (above) the Biddenden
Dole, or Maids' Charity, is distributed from the former
workhouse. The charity was supposedly set up in the 12th
century by the Siamese twins Eliza and Mary Chulkhurst.
The sisters left the parish 20 acres of land, the income from
which was to provide for the annual dole of bread, cheese
and beer, though the beer was eventually dropped. The
photograph shows a parishioner receiving her bread and
cheese in 1952, as she had done for 18 years.*

HARVEST TIME

*The busiest time of the farming calendar
when, before the invention of machine
harvesters, all were required to give a
helping hand. Scything beaten-down oats on
Cleeve Hill near Cheltenham (right).
Gleaners in a field in Essex (above).
In time-honoured custom families were
allowed into the fields to pick up ears of corn
left behind by the harvesters.*

HARVEST FESTIVAL

Thanks were offered for the safe gathering in of the crops at Harvest Festival. All the village would contribute flowers and produce to decorate the church, and favourite harvest hymns would be sung. These scenes were photographed in the village of Cassington in Oxfordshire.

H A R V E S T   S U P P E R

*After the thankgiving service, a harvest supper would be
given by the farmers to thank all the harvesters and to
celebrate the end of a period of gruelling work. A harvest
supper in the village of Mabe in Cornwall.*

AUTUMN WORK

*Preserving, pickling and bottling: women
often gathered to do this work together,
particularly during and after the Second
World War when the Women's Institute was
made responsible for preserving as much
fruit as possible and increasing food
production. Preparing fruit for jam in 1941
in the village of Sandhurst in Kent (above).
In Ashton-under-Edge in the Vale of
Evesham in 1948 (left) women make their
way to the village hall to make use of the
community's fruit-canning machine.*

WINTER VILLAGE

*Village scenes in winter: a farmer at Hoyland Swaine in
Yorkshire (above left) sets out on horseback to collect
provisions from nearby Penistone, while milk is delivered
by sledge in Woodmancote, Gloucestershire (below left).
A farmer herds his cows to be milked morning and
evening, whatever the weather (above).*

CHRISTMAS CUSTOMS

*Combining the Christian with the pagan, as
with so many ancient traditions: the
Christmas mummers in Marshfield in
Gloucestershire (right). Mummers' plays date
from medieval times and survived the
Puritans' ban on them. They are particularly
associated with Christmas, with rehearsals
starting on All-Hallows' Eve. Traditionally
they include a duel between St George and a
Turkish knight, suggesting that they found
their form at the time of the Crusades. The
costumes are known as 'disguises' and it is
essential that they mask the identity of the
players. At Ewelme in Oxfordshire (above)
the verger adjusts the lantern as the choir
prepares to go carol-singing.*

THE NEW YEAR

Wassailing the apple trees to make them fruit abundantly, a rite that used to be performed in orchards all over the south and west of England. Some Somerset villagers are photographed in the 1930s (above), taking part in the Twelfth Night ritual. The owner of the trees and his men go down to the orchard after dark with shot-guns and cider; the drink is poured round the roots of one of the trees and shots are fired through its branches; and the wassail song 'Here's to thee, auld apple tree' is sung. Every year on January 6th the Hood Game is played in the village of Haxey in Lincolnshire (right). Its origins are lost in the mists of time, but according to legend it was first played in the 13th century after Lady Mowbray lost her scarlet hood in a gale while riding from Haxey to Westwoodside. The players are the 12 'Boggons', who must wear red coats and red flowers in their hats.

80

EASTER FESTIVITIES

In the Yorkshire village of Midgley boys perform the Pace-egg Play in 1939. It is an Easter version of the ancient mumming play and, as so often with old folk customs, the participants are dressed in fantastic costumes and wear paint on their faces. The boys in the photograph are nearly all wearing clogs.

MAY DAY

May Day celebrations are probably the best known of all the old English customs. Traditionally, young men and girls went out from the village into the countryside to gather boughs of blossom before dawn on May 1st and returned to decorate their houses and the church. Later there was dancing and singing, and hobbyhorses and Jacks-in-the-Green made their appearance. Traditions varied from village to village, with some surviving longer than others. Boys at Heamoor in Cornwall blow horns at dawn on May morning (below left); people used to complain that boys blew horns all night long on what was sometimes called 'Mischief Night'. A May Day procession at Elstow Green in Bedfordshire (above left). At Eastington in Gloucestershire in 1936 the May Queen takes her customary drink at the memorial to Queen Victoria's jubilee (above).

SUMMER CUSTOMS

*The custom of decorating wells and springs flourished in the
Derbyshire villages. Once upon a time the decorations consisted of
simple wreaths and garlands, but by the early 19th century
elaborate floral pictures and texts began to appear.
They were made by pressing leaves, grass, moss, petals, or
anything natural, onto a screen covered with damp clay.
This scene (left) was photographed at Tissington in Derbyshire,
where five wells were dressed and blessed every year on Ascension
Day since at least 1615. That year the water at Tissington
continued to flow in spite of a severe drought, and the
decorations were put up as a thanksgiving. At Yarnton in
Oxfordshire (above) the uncut grass on the meadows was
auctioned every summer, fetching 1/- an acre in 1933, when this
photograph was taken. The hay was allotted to villagers by
means of named balls drawn out of a bag.*

WHIT MONDAY

Whit, or 'White', Sunday is one of the main feasts of the Church. It used to be followed by several days of jollifications and the drinking of special Whitsun ale; Whit Monday was proclaimed an official holiday in 1871. The day became a popular one for fairs, as shown in this scene of the band marching down the village street at South Harting in Sussex.

COUNTRY DANCES

Morris dancing was a favourite form of entertainment at Whitsun. Bampton in Oxfordshire is believed have had the longest unbroken tradition of Morris dancing in the country, claiming to be more than 500 years old. Here (below), the dancers are accompanied by the treasurer, who carries a cake impaled on a flower-decorated sword, small slices of which are bought to bring good fortune and fertility. Another ancient and traditional dance is the Horn Dance of Abbot's Bromley in Staffordshire (above right), which is performed in September on the Monday of the local Wakes Week. The dancers include a team of six men wearing reindeer horns, a fool, a man-woman, a hobbyhorse, a bowman and musicians.

VILLAGE CRICKET

Cricket has always brought together men of all ages in the neighbourhood, and from all walks of life. Scenes in Frocester in Gloucestershire in 1944: the team searches for a lost ball (above) and batsmen wait their turn in the 'pavilion' (right), a nearby cartshed. The cricket club in the village of Kenton boasts superior facilities (left).

CARNIVALS AND FÊTES

*At some summer events the English enthusiasm for
dressing-up could be given full rein: the fortune-teller
at Flaunden in Hertfordshire (below right),
the Carnival King and Queen at Denham in
Buckinghamshire (above right), and the 18th century
re-created at Hadley in Hertfordshire (below).*

CHURCH BELLS

*Most country churches have six bells, with their own bell-
ringing customs: an evening curfew, a bell at five in the
morning during Lent or, on the death of a parishioner, a
toll for each year of his life. Here the bell-ringers in the
village of Shebbear in north Devon ring a peal of sixties
on thirds to frighten away the Devil.*